Electronic Keyboard Grade 3

Pieces & Technical Work
for Trinity Guildhall examinations

2011-2013

Published by
Trinity College London
89 Albert Embankment
London SE1 7TP UK

T +44 (0)20 7820 6100
F +44 (0)20 7820 6161
E music@trinityguildhall.co.uk
www.trinityguildhall.co.uk

Minuet in G

Ludwig van Beethoven
arr. Nancy Litten

Voices: Strings (dual voice Piano)/Bassoon* (dual voice Flute)
Style: Waltz

* sounding octave lower.
The repeat must be played in the examination.

PLEASE SET UP FOR THE NEXT PIECE

This piece is published under licence from Nancy Litten.

The Swan

from *Carnival of the Animals*

Camille Saint-Saëns
arr. Victoria Proudler

Voices: Cello*/Strings
Style: Waltz (choose a style with quaver movement)

* sounding octave lower.

PLEASE SET UP FOR THE NEXT PIECE

The Sun Whose Rays Are All Ablaze

from *The Mikado*

Gilbert and Sullivan
arr. Nigel Fletcher

Voices: Harp/Flute/Strings
Style: Waltz (gentle)

PLEASE SET UP FOR THE NEXT PIECE

In the Hall of the Mountain King

from *Peer Gynt Suite* no. 1 op. 46

Edvard Grieg
arr. Joanna Clarke

Voices: Bassoon* (dual voice Pizz. Strings)
Style: Hip Hop

* sounding octave lower.
** Number of bars depends on length of ending used.

Coincide last bar with Ending
PLEASE SET UP FOR THE NEXT PIECE
This piece is published under licence from Joanna Clarke.

Sea Shanty and Hornpipe

Own Interpretation

Voices: _____

Style: _____

Traditional
arr. Nigel Fletcher

PLEASE SET UP FOR THE NEXT PIECE

La puesta del sol

Natalie Bleicher

Boogie on the Blues

Voices: Piano/Brass
Style: Swing

Victoria Proudler

* The dynamics in bars 13-14, 17-18 and 21-22 apply to the right hand only.

PLEASE SET UP FOR THE NEXT PIECE

This piece is published under licence from Victoria Proudler.

Why did you leave me?

Nigel Fletcher

Voices: Piano/Strings (dual voice Brass)
Style: Slow Ballad/Slow Rock ⏰ (or ⏰)

PLEASE SET UP FOR THE NEXT PIECE

Bhang-a-ragga

Bhangra Moderne

Kuljit Bhamra

Voices: Flute/Banjo
Style: Ragga (or 8 Beat Pop if Ragga not available)

♩ = 80

Rhythm on
Flute

PLEASE SET UP FOR THE NEXT PIECE

The Sarah Jane Adventures

Murray Gold
arr. Nigel Fletcher

Voice: Strings (dual voice Trumpet)
Style: Big Band

THEME FROM THE SIMPSONS™

from the Twentieth Century Fox Television Series THE SIMPSONS

Music by
DANNY ELFMAN

Moderately fast

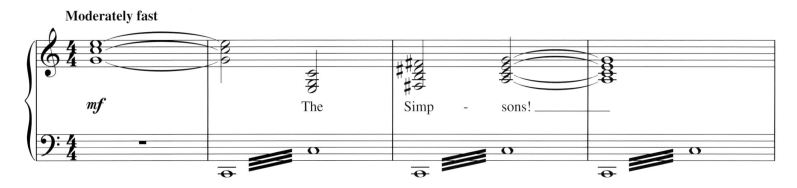

mf   The   Simp   -   sons! _____

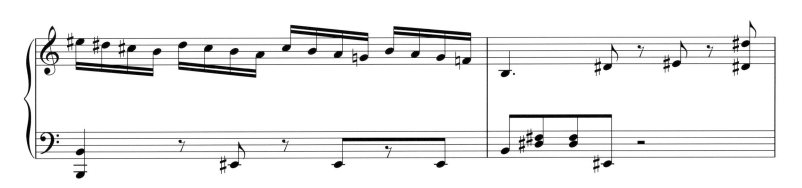

HL00352981

EXCLUSIVELY DISTRIBUTED BY

7777 W. BLUEMOUND RD. P.O. BOX 13819 MILWAUKEE, WI 53213

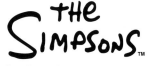

12-06
U.S. $3.95

0 73999 47253 0

Technical Work

All sections i) to iii) to be prepared. Sections i) and ii) must be performed from memory; the music may be used for Section iii).

i) Scales

The following scales to be performed in piano voice with auto-accompaniment off, hands together (unless otherwise stated),
♩ = 90, *legato* and **mf**:

E♭ and A major (two octaves)
C and F♯ minor (two octaves): candidate's choice of *either* harmonic *or* melodic *or* natural minor
E♭ major contrary motion scale (two octaves)
Chromatic scale in similar motion starting on E♭ (two octaves)
Minor pentatonic scale starting on C and G, right hand only (one octave)

E♭ major scale (two octaves)

A major scale (two octaves)

C minor scale: harmonic (two octaves)

C minor scale: melodic (two octaves)

C minor scale: natural (two octaves)

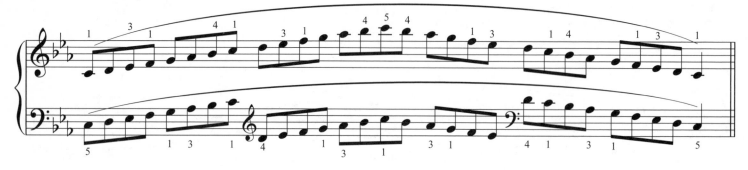

F# minor scale: harmonic (two octaves)

F# minor scale: melodic (two octaves)

F# minor scale: natural (two octaves)

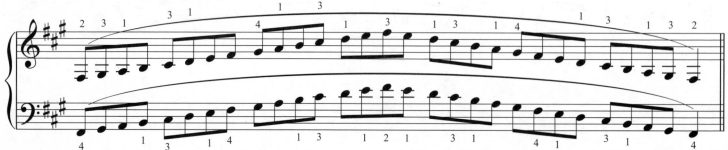

Eb major contrary motion scale (two octaves)

Chromatic scale in similar motion starting on Eb (two octaves)

Minor pentatonic scale starting on C (one octave)

Right hand

Minor pentatonic scale starting on G (one octave)

Right hand

please turn over

ii) Chord knowledge

The following to be performed with the left hand in piano voice with auto-accompaniment off:

Triad of E♭ and A major, C and F♯ minor (root position, first and second inversions)
Chord of E♭⁷ and A⁷ (root position, first, second and third inversion)

E♭ major

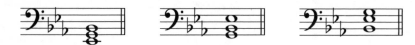

A major

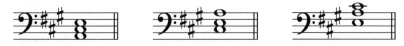

C minor

F♯ minor

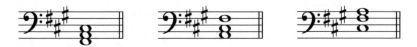

E♭⁷

A⁷

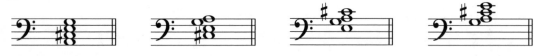

iii) Exercises

Candidate to prepare all three exercises.

1. Cool It! – bass clef reading and finger dexterity

Voice: Honky Tonk Piano
Style: Swing

♩ = 90

Accomp. off
Rhythm on

2. Sunshine and Shadow – arpeggios and chord use [fingered chords must be used]

Voice: Violin
Style: Ballad

♩ = 90

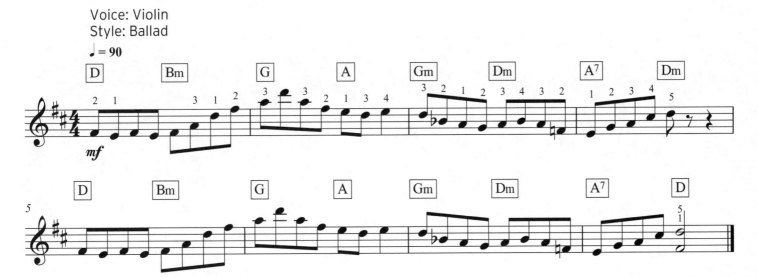

3. A Little Waltz – using keyboard functions

Voice: Violin (dual voice*)
Style: Waltz

Add dual voice
To Accomp. B

* Candidate's choice of dual voice.